SUPER STRUCTURES OF THE WORLD

SKYSCRAPERS

San Diego • Detroit • New York • San Francisco • Cleveland • New Haven, Conn. • Waterville, Maine • London • Munich

© 2004 by Blackbirch Press™. Blackbirch Press™ is an imprint of The Gale Group, Inc., a division of Thomson Learning, Inc.

Blackbirch Press™ and Thomson Learning™ are trademarks used herein under license.

For more information, contact
The Gale Group, Inc.
27500 Drake Rd.
Farmington Hills, MI 48331-3535
Or you can visit our Internet site at http://www.gale.com

ALL RIGHTS RESERVED
No part of this work covered by the copyright hereon may be reproduced or used in any form or by any means—graphic, electronic, or mechanical, including photocopying, recording, taping, Web distribution or information storage retrieval systems—without the written permission of the publisher.

Every effort has been made to trace the owners of copyrighted material.

Photo credits: cover, pages all © Discovery Communications, Inc. except for pages 3, 12-13, 46 © Blackbirch Press Archives; page 8 © Hulton Archive; pages 20, 28 © Cesar Pelli & Associates; pages 34-35 © CORBIS. Image on bottom banner © PhotoDisc

Discovery Communications, Discovery Communications logo, TLC (The Learning Channel), TLC (The Learning Channel) logo, Animal Planet, and the Animal Planet logo are trademarks of Discovery Communications Inc., used under license.

LIBRARY OF CONGRESS CATALOGING-IN-PUBLICATION DATA

Skyscrapers / Elaine Pascoe, editor.
    p. cm. — (Super structures of the world)
Summary: Examines the history of the world's tallest buildings, including some of the challenges faced in design and construction and how their builders tested the limits of technology.
Includes bibliographical references and index.
  ISBN 1-56711-869-0 (hardback : alk. paper) — ISBN 1-4103-0192-3 (pbk. alk. paper)
  1. Skyscrapers—Juvenile literature. 2. Architecture, Modern—20th century—Juvenile literature. [1. Skyscrapers.] I. Pascoe, Elaine. II. Series.

NA6230.S48 2004
720'.483—dc21
                                              2003009272

Printed in China
10 9 8 7 6 5 4 3 2 1

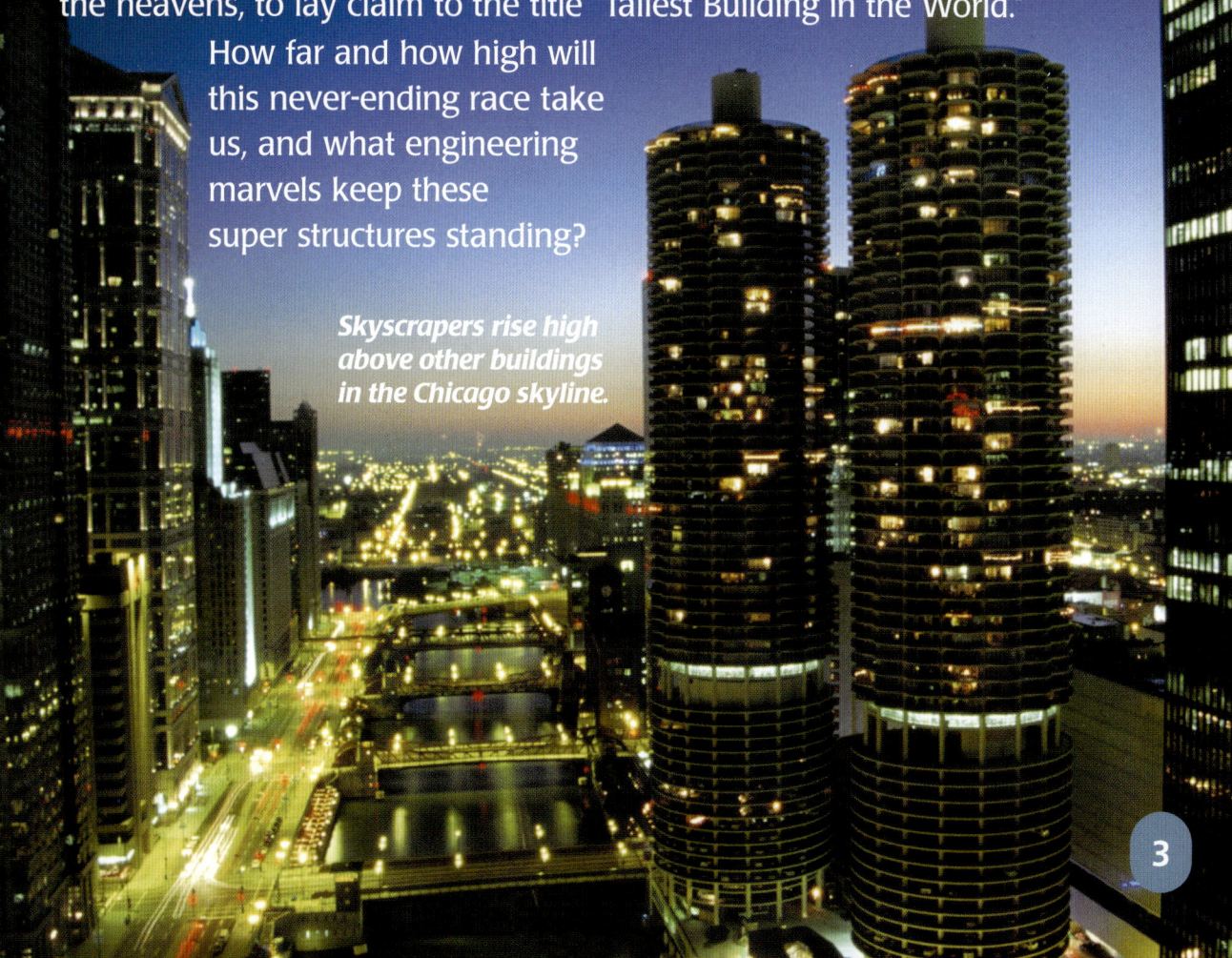

SUPER STRUCTURES OF THE WORLD
SKYSCRAPERS

They seem to defy gravity. Forged from concrete and steel, skyscrapers loom over today's urban jungle. They embody the souls of those who built them, the strength and courage of high steelworkers, and the danger of such a passion. As gracefully as they rise, skyscrapers collapse with unparalleled devastation.

Yet, in the face of potential disaster, architects continue to design these super structures higher and higher. It has become a race toward the heavens, to lay claim to the title "Tallest Building in the World." How far and how high will this never-ending race take us, and what engineering marvels keep these super structures standing?

Skyscrapers rise high above other buildings in the Chicago skyline.

Engineers in Japan, like many others elsewhere, have no choice but to build up. Land is scarce and real estate prices are soaring. To meet the needs of a growing population, skyscrapers are the only answer. The JR Central Towers in Nagoya, one of Japan's largest buildings, encloses more than 4.5 million square feet. Built in the middle of a crowded city and on top of a busy train station, this building tested every facet of modern engineering.

Right: Some countries, like Japan, have no land left to build on. Instead, they build upward with more skyscrapers.

Left: The growth of Japan's population is constant and builders accommodate the country's many people with the construction of more skyscrapers.

In Kuala Lumpur, the capital of Malaysia, space is not an issue. Land for construction abounds. Yet this city is home to a modern 1,483-foot skyscraper, the Petronas Towers, an amazing structure of glass and steel. With eighty-eight floors and one hundred foot spires, these twin towers are a monument to architect Cesar Pelli's dreams. Completed in 1999, the Petronas Towers earned the coveted crown as the world's tallest building.

Above right: Kuala Lumpur, Malaysia, houses the tallest building in the world—a coveted title among architects.

Right: The Petronas Twin Towers reach a height of 1,483 feet and enclose eighty-eight stories within each tower.

CONQUERING GRAVITY

Whether built out of need or inspiration, constructing these mammoth skyscrapers relies heavily upon technological advances. First, skyscrapers, architects and engineers had to conquer the force of gravity.

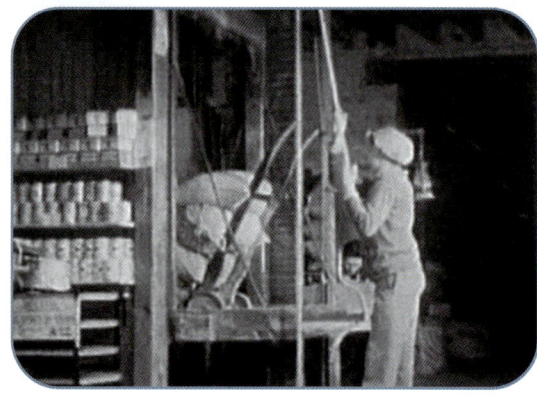

Left: The Petronas Towers are mammoth super structures in today's world. Bottom left: Elisha Otis created a safety brake that eventually led to the first modern elevator. Below: In the mid-1800s workers had to use a precarious pulley system for vertical transportation.

During the mid-1800's, the only means of vertical transportation other than climbing stairs was a rope-and-pulley system driven by a steam engine. However, the system was too dangerous for passengers, since the ropes often broke.

Frustrated, Elisha Otis invented a safety brake that locked the platform to its guides. In 1852, what seems a minor invention paved the way for the modern elevator. Slowly, the public began to trust the Otis elevator. Upper-level floors became fashionable and profitable, as architects quickly adopted this new means of vertical transportation.

Top: Otis's invention solved the problem of vertical transportation and allowed taller buildings to be constructed.

Left: Elevators and upper-level floors quickly became stylish in the nineteenth century.

Even with the use of an elevator, buildings rising above two hundred feet remained a dream. The building materials of the day, bricks, stones, and mortar, were simply too heavy to allow great heights. But in 1885, with the invention of the steel-cage structure, the modern skyscraper was born.

The steel cage supports the building like a skeleton, bearing most of the weight of the building. It is no longer necessary to support the building with massive walls. The exterior, or "skin", of the building can now be made of much lighter materials, such as glass and aluminum. The result is an explosion of buildings taller than anyone has ever seen.

Without this technology, skyscrapers rising above twenty stories would not be possible. It is the backbone of every tall building's design, even the eight hundred foot JR Central Towers in Nagoya. That skyscraper is made up of three steel cages. One forms the base of the building, while two rise up within each tower.

Opposite page: The steel-cage structure allowed workers to use materials that are easier to haul, like glass and aluminum, in construction.

Above: Because the steel cage provided a strong skeleton for a building, massive walls were no longer needed.

For more than one hundred years, the steel-cage structure has enabled engineers to build skyscrapers higher and higher. In Malaysia, more than 26,000 tons of steel and 160,000 cubic meters of concrete were used in the framing of the Petronas Towers. But at what altitude do skyscrapers become too dangerous? Almost sixty years ago, a deadly incident hinted at the risks.

Above: The steel-cage structure permits tall buildings to rise from the ground like never before.

Below: The Petronas Towers has more than twenty-six thousand tons of steel in its frame.

Above: While the steel-cage structure allows buildings to go higher and higher, there are still risks at such heights.

In 1945 the tallest building in the world was New York's Empire State Building, rising an incredible 1,250 feet. But then came a jarring reminder of the dangers of building so high. A B-25 Mitchell bomber, trying to reach a nearby airport, crashed into the Empire State Building. The pilot and thirteen others died. But the building sustained little damage and was open for business two days later. Its ability to survive a collision with a World Word II bomber seemed to validate modern engineering technology. A skyscraper building boom swept across the United States. In 1974 the Sears Tower, rising 1,454 feet above Chicago, grabbed the title of the tallest building in the world.

Below: When a bomber crashed into the Empire State Building in New York in 1945, the resulting damage confirmed one risk of skyscrapers.

Above: At 1,250 feet, the Empire State Building was the tallest building in the world until 1974, when construction of the Sears Tower in Chicago reached completion.

Skyscraper construction in the United States has steadily declined since the early 1970s. But a new skyscraper building boom has spread throughout the Pacific Rim. Once again cities are vying to have the world's tallest building. Only time will tell if this architectural pursuit will prove deadly. Unavoidable forces threaten the engineers of Pacific Rim skyscrapers like the JR Central Towers and the Petronas Towers. They are building in one of the most seismic active regions in the world, where the threat of a major earthquake is constant. How safe will these new structures be when a violent earthquake shakes their very foundations?

Below: While skyscraper construction has decreased in the United States, cities in the Pacific Rim are building more and more of these super structures.

This spread: The Singapore skyline is one example of how cities in the Pacific Rim are contributing to a skyscraper boom, despite major threats such as earthquakes.

DANGER FROM BELOW

On September 19, 1985, a killer earthquake registering 8.0 on the Richter scale rocked Mexico City. More than ten thousand people were killed, and more than one hundred thousand left homeless. The quake damaged nearly three thousand structures, and four hundred totally collapsed. For the city's towering skyscrapers, once a symbol of modern Mexico, this quake was devastating. During the ninety seconds of shaking, some skyscrapers swayed six feet, three times farther than what is considered safe. Neighboring buildings slammed into each other, causing major damage.

Left: More than four hundred buildings collapsed in the 8.0 earthquake. Skyscrapers swayed three times farther than the safe limit.

Right: Newscasters are interrupted on air by a major earthquake in Mexico City in 1985.

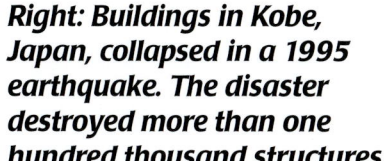

Right: Buildings in Kobe, Japan, collapsed in a 1995 earthquake. The disaster destroyed more than one hundred thousand structures.

Left: The 7.2 earthquake that rocked Kobe destroyed more than 20 percent of Kobe's buildings, including several skyscrapers.

Ten years later, the Japanese city of Kobe was devastated by a 7.2 earthquake. More than one hundred thousand buildings were destroyed. Another eighty thousand were severely damaged. And in downtown Kobe, home to most of the city's skyscrapers, 60 percent of the buildings sustained significant structural damage. More than 20 percent were completely destroyed.

But the devastating failures in both Mexico City and Kobe have provided the building community with valuable insights. When the earth moves, the skyscraper's center of gravity becomes offset. The top of the building tends to lag behind the base, putting more stress on the columns. The building can be permanently damaged or even collapse. But using computers to simulate the shaking a building sustains during a major earthquake, researchers discovered that strengthening a skyscraper's foundation may prevent these structural failures.

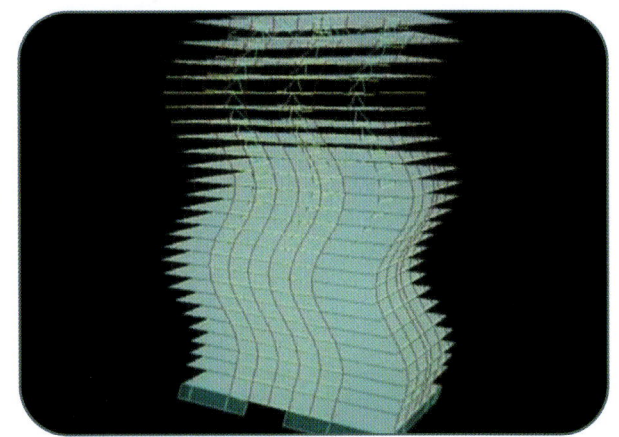

Above: A digitized skyscraper shakes during a computer-simulated earthquake. This experiment showed that such disasters can be averted if the foundations of these structures are strengthened.

Left: Researchers discovered that a skyscraper's center of gravity is altered during an earthquake, which puts more pressure on the columns of the building and could cause it to collapse.

In Nagoya, Japan, only 140 miles from Kobe, the engineers of the JR Central Towers put this research to the test. Architect Paul Katz designed the strongest foundation ever constructed for a skyscraper. To anchor the building, engineers drove 125-foot steel beams 60 feet into the bedrock. Those columns were encased in steel reinforcement bars and concrete, becoming the base frame of the building and bearing the majority of its weight.

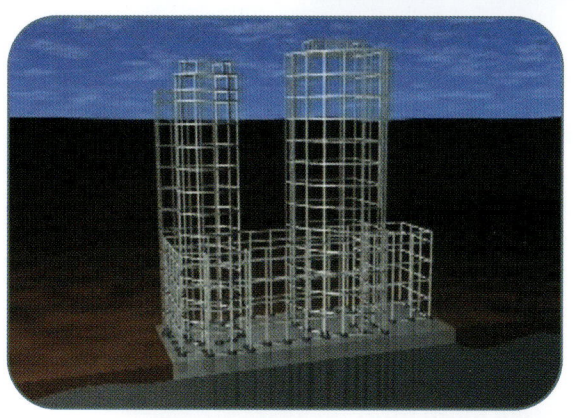

Top right: JR Central, a skyscraper in Nagoya, Japan, now has a strong foundation to secure the building to the ground. Middle: Computer research gave engineers an idea of how to anchor the building's columns to remove some of the pressure. Bottom: The new design created a new base frame of steel and concrete to take on most of the weight.

More than 1.5 million cubic feet of concrete was poured around the steel piles, creating what is called a "mat-slab foundation"—a huge block of concrete, more than 20 feet thick. Finally, the steel structure of the skyscraper aboveground was bolted to the foundation piles below. The mat-slab foundation prevents the steel-cage structure aboveground from swaying too far during an earthquake.

Above: The mat-slab foundation was constructed of steel piles covered in concrete. Bottom left: The steel structure of the skyscraper was bolted into the mat-slab foundation, which protects the aboveground structure in the case of an earthquake. Bottom right: Blocks of concrete more than twenty feet thick were used in this construction method.

The taller the building, the larger the foundation necessary. Because of the limited space surrounding the skyscraper, the JR Central Towers foundation was excavated in an underground cavern. The Petronas Towers foundation spread out, covering more than one and a half acres— one of the largest mat slab foundations ever constructed.

Before a drop of concrete was poured, the bedrock at the proposed site of the twin giants became an issue of concern for architect Cesar Pelli. The limestone below the site was like Swiss cheese, riddled with holes and cracks. It required drilling the foundation more than four hundred feet underground, or more than six times the depth needed at the JR Central Towers.

Top: Cesar Pelli, the architect who designed the Petronas Towers, designed one of the largest mat-slab foundations ever created as the base of the Twin Towers. Right: The foundation for the Petronas Towers had to be drilled more than four hundred feet underground to prepare for the massive structure built atop it.

Once the foundation piles were in, more than seventy thousand tons of concrete were cast into the mat slab. Pouring around-the-clock, the work continued for three straight days. It was the largest single pour of concrete ever done, and the timing had to be perfect. If one side of the foundation was to dry and settle before the entire job was completed, an uneven base would result. If the skyscraper was built on an uneven base, the building's weight distribution would be uneven. It would be off balance; an earthquake could easily bring it tumbling down.

Will these enormous mat-slab foundations safeguard the buildings during a major earthquake? Their engineers believe so, but others are skeptical. They note that a similar faith in building design guided engineers in Los Angeles for years. Their faith was shattered in January 17, 1994, when the magnitude 6.8 Northridge earthquake struck southern California.

Left: Several buildings were severely damaged during the 1994 Northridge earthquake in southern California.

Opposite page: The massive site of the Petronas Towers included more than seventy thousand tons of concrete in the mat-slab foundation alone.

In some areas, engineering failed and structures crumbled. None of Los Angeles' skyscrapers collapsed. But an inspection of their inner steel-cage frames revealed major damage in the welds connecting the vertical columns to horizontal beams in many buildings. The Northridge quake was short, only twenty seconds. Laboratory tests showed that had the shaking lasted as long as those in Mexico City or Kobe, the cracked beams would have ruptured completely, causing structural failure in many of these buildings.

Top right: While no skyscrapers collapsed in the Los Angeles quake, cracked beams appeared in the structures upon inspection. Above left: Because the earthquake was short, the damage was minimal compared to longer quakes in Japan and Mexico. Above right: If the quake had lasted much longer, some skyscrapers may have collapsed.

The sobering news sent shock waves throughout the engineering world. The steel-cage structure, once thought safe, was vulnerable during a strong earthquake. Engineers turned to new technology to prevent such stress-induced failures. Dampers, devices installed within the diagonal trusses of the steel-cage structure, reduce shaking during a quake much like shock absorbers in a car. A skyscraper with dampers can absorb up to three times more energy produced by an earthquake than a building without them. The longer a quake lasts, the more effective a damper can be, absorbing more energy with each shock wave.

Tall building engineers were quick to adopt the damper technology. Fourteen were installed in Petronas' Twin Towers, and six in the JR Central Towers.

Above and right: A new technological device, called a damper, was developed to absorb shock waves in buildings during an earthquake.

DANGER FROM ABOVE

Skyscrapers face another, more immediate danger—wind. The taller a building rises, the stronger the winds it faces. Skyscraper design must take into account these turbulent forces. In fact, wind is what drives the design of very tall buildings.

Left: Tall buildings are susceptible to strong winds and need to be flexible enough to bend with the wind's force.

Right: Wind is another risk factor architects must consider when they design skyscrapers.

Wind pushes against a building like the sail of a boat. In order to withstand these blustery forces, a tall building must be flexible enough to bend and absorb some of the wind, while still remaining rigid enough not to topple. The JR Central Towers provides a model of how this balance is achieved. The three inner steel cages provide flexibility, allowing the towers to sway up to four and a half feet in strong winds, while the rigid central core of reinforced concrete adds the stability needed to prevent the tower from snapping in winds gusting up to 175 miles per hour. However, as skyscrapers are built higher and higher, they encounter stronger winds and are required to sway even farther to remain upright. Architects must now deal with a whole new design problem. On top floors, how much swaying and vibration can people tolerate?

Top: This computer model shows how balance is achieved to allow buildings to sway with the wind and still remain upright.

Above left: Three inner steel cages supply flexibility and a concrete central core stabilizes the skyscraper.

If a swaying skyscraper can cause motion sickness in average high wind conditions, then the occupants of the Petronas Towers had better prepare for a wild ride. Reaching nearly fifteen hundred feet, the Twin Towers are designed to withstand the devastating winds that strike the region. These swirling gusts can reach over ninety miles per hour. Each tower needs to sway almost three feet just to prevent a structural collapse.

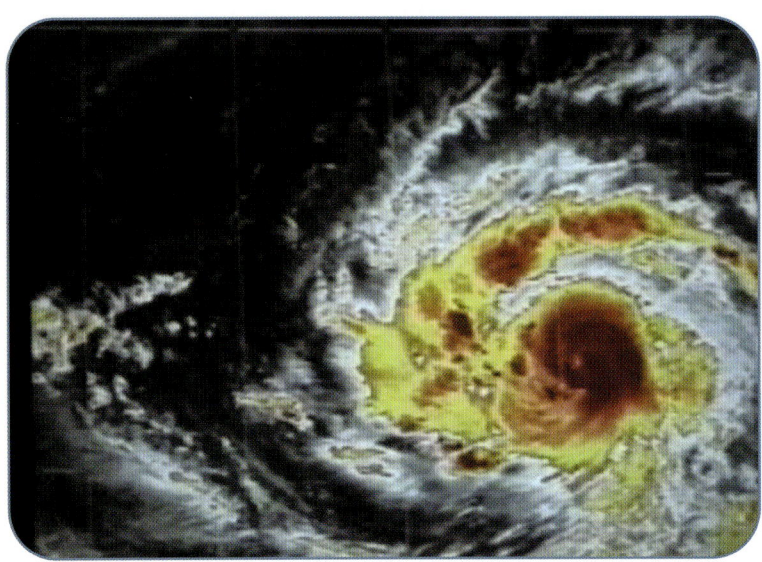

Top left: The Petronas Towers are designed to withstand Malaysia's powerful winds.

Left: Swirling winds over Malaysia can reach speeds of more than ninety miles per hour.

The design challenge at Petronas was compounded by a bridge that connects the two towers at their fortieth and forty-first floors. Architect Cesar Pelli envisioned the bridge as a symbol, marking a gate to the sky. It would also serve as an escape route in case of fires or emergencies. But it clashed with the towers' physical reality. If swirling winds pushed the Twin Towers in different directions, the nine hundred-ton bridge might snap apart, plummeting more than six hundred feet onto a crowded walkway below.

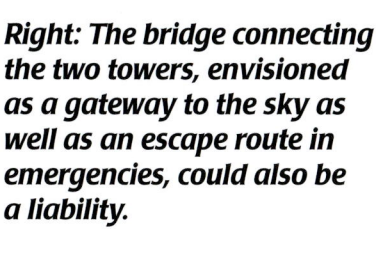

Right: The bridge connecting the two towers, envisioned as a gateway to the sky as well as an escape route in emergencies, could also be a liability.

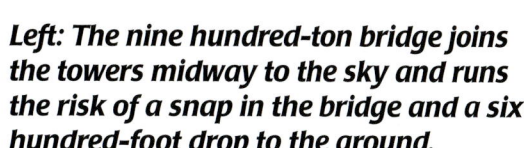

Left: The nine hundred-ton bridge joins the towers midway to the sky and runs the risk of a snap in the bridge and a six hundred-foot drop to the ground.

This page: Engineers of the Pertronas Towers used earthquake technology and designed the sky bridge's support legs to work as dampers.

To solve this unique design problem, engineers borrowed something from earthquake technology, dampers. The sky bridge's support legs, 117 feet long and weighing sixty tons each, are in essence enormous dampers that help absorb the vibrations created when both buildings sway. To prevent these legs from snapping off when the towers sway in opposite directions, each leg is attached to a rotating plate that can twist at least forty-five degrees in any direction. As a result, the damper legs absorb the torque and sway while the bridge's interior support system remains unaffected.

Above left: The support legs of the sky bridge are anchored to rotation plates. These plates swivel to help the support legs absorb vibrations when the buildings sway in opposite directions.

Left: This digital image depicts how the damper legs of the sky bridge will sway, allowing the interior support system of the bridge to remain stationary.

NEW THREATS

Designed to survive the battering of high winds and the violent shaking of earthquakes, modern skyscrapers seem indestructible. But where nature might fail, man has succeeded. On September 11, 2001, terrorists flew two hijacked airliners into the Twin Towers of New York's World Trade Center, killing nearly three thousand people and destroying both towers. The attack ushered in a dark new reality. The threat of terrorism had finally come home.

Right: On September 11, 2001, terrorists introduced a new threat to skyscrapers when they flew two airplanes into the World Trade Center's Twin Towers in New York City.

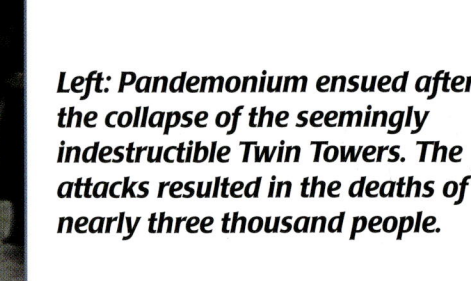

Left: Pandemonium ensued after the collapse of the seemingly indestructible Twin Towers. The attacks resulted in the deaths of nearly three thousand people.

Chillingly, a prelude to the September 11 attack occurred on February 26, 1993, when a bomb was set off in a parking structure below the World Trade Center's 110-story Twin Towers. The blast killed six people, injured more than one thousand, and caused millions of dollars worth of damage. It did not bring down the towers or even cause severe damage to the structure of the buildings. But it did point out a major hazard: fire.

Top: A previous terrorist attack occurred at the World Trade Center in 1993 when a car bomb went off in a parking garage below the skyscrapers. Above left: Rescue workers acted quickly to save the thousands of people inside the Twin Towers. Right: The Twin Towers of the World Trade Center stood 110-stories-tall before the September 11 attack.

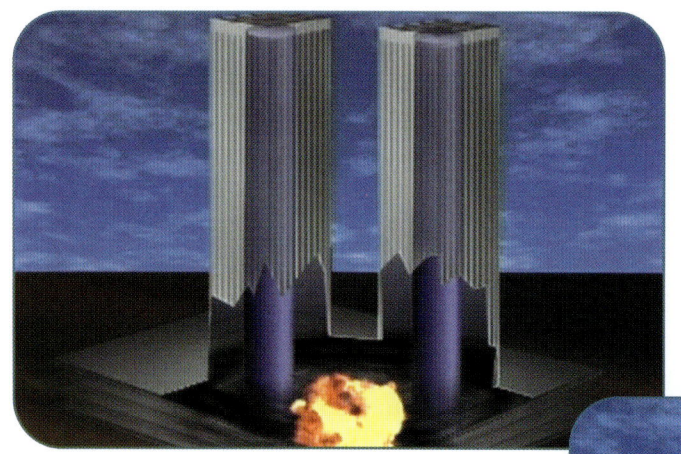

Left: *A digital depiction of the 1993 bombing shows how fire and smoke quickly moved upward into the towers.*

Right: *The towers did not collapse in 1993 because their steel cage skeletons absorbed the blast of the bomb.*

   The Twin Towers acted like giant chimneys, sucking fire and smoke upward. Thousands of people were trapped in darkness. Emergency systems failed, smoke filled the towers, and people smashed windows in a frantic search for air. They survived because the building stayed up. The steel cage skeleton absorbed the force of the bomb and prevented its collapse by distributing the blast shock throughout the entire frame. But the inner columns, designed to give the towers their rigidity, became the vertical conduits for the deadly fire and smoke. Eventually, firefighters were able to release the trapped smoke by smashing windows on the lower floors and cutting air holes in the roof of the towers.

During the ensuing investigation, engineers discovered that the building's emergency fire and sprinkler systems had been knocked off-line, allowing the spread of the fire and smoke. Engineers were handed a new challenge—developing an advanced infrastructure to ensure that the air, water, and fire systems can function under extreme situations.

Right: Firefighters worked to save the World Trade Center. Their job was made harder because the explosion damaged emergency and sprinkler systems.

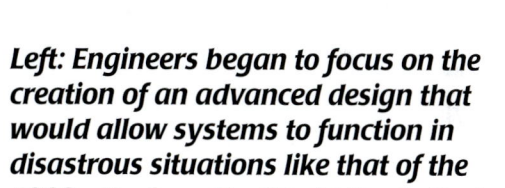

Left: Engineers began to focus on the creation of an advanced design that would allow systems to function in disastrous situations like that of the 1993 attack on the World Trade Center.

This spread: The unforeseen attacks on September 11, 2001, led to the collapse of the Twin Towers, once thought of as invincible super structures.

NEW SOLUTIONS

For the engineers of the Petronas Towers, simply providing water to the entire building was a huge obstacle. Over six hundred pounds of pressure are needed to pump water to the pinnacle of this skyscraper, nearly fifteen hundred feet into the sky. Attaching a faucet or sprinkler to such highly pressurized water would be like trying to drink from the end of a firefighter's hose. To solve this problem, engineers decide to pump water to the very top of the building and then let it cascade down to maintenance floors (on the seventh, forty-third, and eighty-first floors), losing its pressure as it trickles down. From the maintenance floors, pumps distribute the water throughout the tower. These control areas also handle the air and electrical distribution for the floors in their zone. If, during a fire or explosion, one of these maintenance floors is destroyed, the other two can operate independently to suppress any fire and ventilate any smoke.

Left: Engineers created a system to pump water to the top of the Petronas Towers through the sprinklers in case of a fire.

Right: The JR Central Towers could not be square, as originally designed, because this would interfere with television signals and cause a shadowy double image on TV screens.

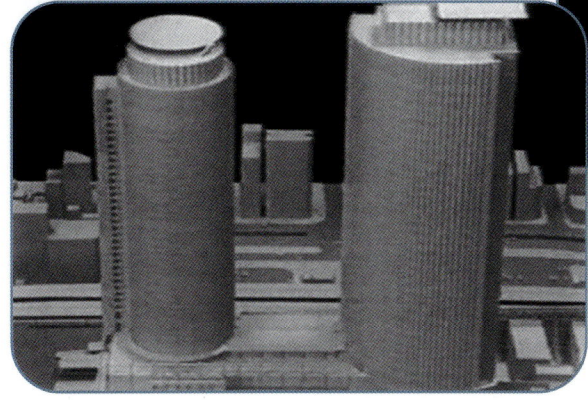

Left: Architects created a new design for JR Central. They used a round shape covered with concrete and ceramic tile.

These high-tech solutions to old problems have made possible the continued growth of modern skyscrapers. Sometimes, the forces that shape designs come from the most unexpected places. In Japan, where cable television has not taken root, most television signals are broadcast through the air. The JR Central Towers were originally designed to be square. However, a rectangular tower would have blocked signals from local TV stations and led to "ghosting"—a shadowy double image on TV screens. The architects were forced to make a multimillion-dollar design change, or suffer the wrath of thousands of television viewers. Besides rounding the shape, they covered the exterior with precast concrete and ceramic tile instead of metal or reflective glass that would cause a broadcast signal to bounce back toward the transmission tower.

Technology does not come cheap. It took seven years to complete the JR Central Towers, at a cost of $1 million dollars a day. But for all the money that is spent, it is the skill of the steelworker that makes all skyscrapers possible.

In Japan the people who work on these tall buildings are some of the most talented and dedicated workers in the world. At the JR Central Towers, the project was viewed as a team job. Each morning, workers performed calisthenics together. A detailed briefing of precisely what work needs to be completed that day followed. The coordination between departments was so precise that the day's work was planned down to the minute.

Above: Construction of the JR Central Towers took seven years, at the cost of $1 million per day.

Right: The workers who built JR Central used special coordination and precise plans to follow a rigid schedule to build the skyscraper.

This dedication paid off for the JR Central Towers. Workers completed an astonishing three floors per week. Elsewhere, the completion of one floor per week is acceptable. But for the many workers on the high steel in Nagoya, being average was not acceptable.

Japanese engineers and workers often train crews building skyscrapers along the Pacific Rim. They came to Kuala Lumpur, and the results stand before all the world to see. Highly skilled workers, technological advances, the dreams of architects— these are the ingredients to build the modern skyscraper. But how high is high enough?

Above left: Engineers and workers managed to complete three floors a week during construction of JR Central. Above right: Because of their experience building Japan's skyscrapers, Japanese engineers trained crews in Kuala Lumpur to build the Petronas Towers.

MEASURING UP

The drive to create the tallest skyscraper in the world has been a one hundred year odyssey, sweeping engineers and architects far beyond their initial dreams. This ambitious race led Cesar Pelli and the engineers of the Petronas Towers to the forefront of modern building design. The

$800 million invested by their backers made the Petronas Towers the tallest building in the world. Or did it? Engineers of the Sears Tower say their building still retains the title, since it has one hundred floors to Petronas' eighty-eight. But Pelli's building includes an enormous spire that tops the building off twenty-two feet higher than the Chicago skyscraper.

Above left: Architects and engineers debate whether the Sears Tower or the Petronas Towers deserves the title of tallest building in the world.

Left: While the Sears Tower has more floors, the spires of the Petronas Towers make the buildings twenty-two feet taller.

This debate will soon be beside the point. While some plans for giant skyscrapers were scaled back after the September 11, 2001, terrorist attacks, others have raced forward. In China work has started on the Shanghai World Financial Center. When finished in 2007 it will loom over this ancient Chinese city at a height of 1,623 feet, taller than both Sears and Petronas. In Taiwan the Taipei Financial Center is planned to stand at 1,671 feet. Plans are under way to add a 1,772-foot tower to a project already under construction in Seoul, South Korea. Proposals for the site of the destroyed World Trade Center in New York City call for a spire rising 1,776 feet. The proposed Center of India Tower in Katangi, India, will be tallest of all, at 2,222 feet.

Architects of proposed skyscrapers in China, Taiwan, South Korea, India, and New York are all vying to create the new "tallest" building.

No structural limit is in sight. Modern buildings are basically thin curtains draped on skeletons of high-stress steel or concrete materials. Columns shift weight to underground substructures in what are, despite their massive appearance, relatively low-density structures. But is there a physical boundary beyond which science can never advance?

Years ago, a mile-high building with atomic-powered elevators connecting over 528 floors was designed by American architect Frank Lloyd Wright. If built, a skyscraper this tall would stand over five times the height of today's tallest structures. In Wright's day, a mile-high building seemed a futuristic folly. But is it still?

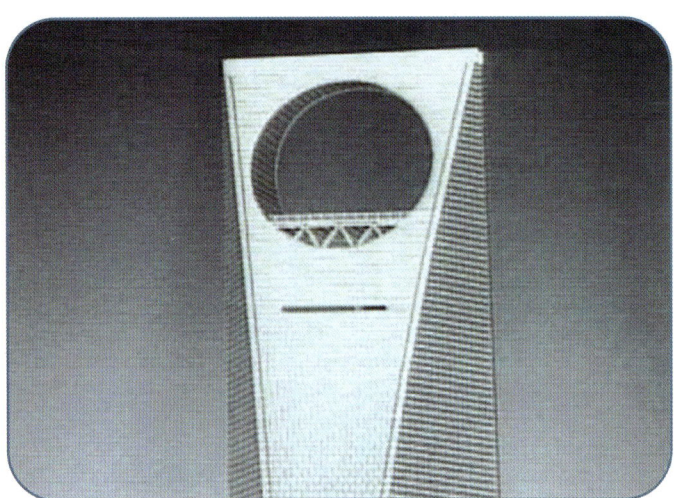

Above: American architect Frank Lloyd Wright designed a building with atomic-powered elevators that would stretch a mile into the sky.

Left: Wright envisioned a mile-high skyscraper with more than 528 floors.

Opposite page: Today's skyscrapers are not the limit. Engineers are still striving to reach greater heights with new designs and buildings.

Left: The skyscraper vision of filmmaker Fritz Lang was made reality in his 1928 film Metropolis, *which created an entire city inside one building.*

Right: New lighter building materials, like ceramics and plastics, enable today's engineers to build skyscrapers that are even taller than those already standing.

As technology continues to advance, engineers now say a mile-high building is possible. New, lighter building materials are the key. Already, ceramics are being used in the exterior walls of buildings such as the JR Central Towers to lighten the total weight of the building and reduce the stress on the foundation. New hybrid materials—alloys, ceramics, plastics, carbon fibers, or mixtures of these—may eventually give rise to skyscrapers taller than anyone has ever seen. These monoliths may resemble the vision of the future in filmmaker Fritz Lang's 1928 *Metropolis*, self-contained cities with offices, apartments, hotels, stores, and transportation in one building.

Since their beginnings, skyscrapers have evoked unexplainable emotions in us, from pride to awe to fear. As architect Cesar Pelli says, "There is something magic and extraordinary in a structure that grows from the ground and moves up and reaches the sky."

Right: Skyscrapers will continue to rise high above city skylines as architects continue to bring their extraordinary visions to life.

Left: Fireworks light up the night sky at the grand opening of a new skyscraper. Cesar Pelli sees these creations as magical, man-made, sky-high super structures.

Perhaps these monuments that we leave behind tell much of the human story itself. They speak with stunning eloquence of our ambition and our brilliance, but also of our frailty. As they puncture the skies above our urban landscape, skyscrapers also punch holes in our preconception of what is possible. What was impossible yesterday now stands before us.

GLOSSARY

Architect a person who designs buildings

Bedrock the solid rock underlying the soil

Damper shock absorber

Engineer professional who determines how to build something and oversees the process

Gravity the natural force of attraction that a celestial body exerts on objects near it

Hybrid a combination of two or more things

Infrastructure the underlying foundation or framework of something

Mat-Slab Foundation a foundation consisting of a large slab of cement over steel piles

Pile a column driven into the ground to support a vertical load

Seismic of, subject to, or caused by an earthquake

Skyscraper a very tall building

Steel-Cage Structure a series of vertical columns and horizontal beams in modern skyscrapers that allows for both flexibility and strength

Torque a force that tends to produce rotation

Truss an assembly of beams that form a rigid framework

INDEX

Altitude, 10
Architects, 3, 6, 7, 25, 37, 39

Building materials
  bricks, 9
  ceramics, 37, 44
  concrete, 10, 17–19, 21, 25, 37, 42
  glass, 5, 9, 37
  hybrid, 44
  plastics, 44
  steel, 5, 10, 17, 42

Center of India Tower, 41
Computers, 16
Costs of buildings, 38, 40

Dampers, 23, 29

Earthquakes, 13, 14–16, 21–23, 29, 30
Elevator, 7, 9, 42
Empire State Building (New York), 11
Engineers, 6, 13, 17, 21, 23, 29, 33, 36

Fire, 31–33, 36
Foundation, 16–19, 21, 44

Gravity, 3, 6, 16

Japan, 4, 15, 16, 17, 22, 37, 38
JR Central Towers (Nagoya, Japan), 4, 9, 13, 17, 19, 23, 25, 37–39, 44

Katz, Paul, 17

Lang, Fritz, 44

Mat-slab foundation, 18–19, 21
Mexico City, 14, 16, 22

Northridge earthquake (California), 21–22

Otis, Elisha, 7

Pacific Rim, 13, 39
Pelli, Cesar, 5, 19, 27, 40, 45
Petronas Towers (Kuala Lumpur, Malaysia), 5, 10, 13, 19, 23, 26, 36, 40, 41
  sky bridge of, 27, 29

Sears Tower (Chicago), 11, 40, 41
Seoul (South Korea), 41
September 11, 2001, attacks, 30, 41
Shanghai World Financial Center (China), 41
Steam engine, 7
Steel cage, 9–10, 18, 22–23, 25, 32
Steelworkers, 3, 38

Taipei Financial Center (Taiwan), 41
Tallest building in the world, 3, 5, 11, 13, 40–41
Television signals, 37
Terrorism, 30, 41

Water systems, 33, 36
Wind, 24–27, 30
World Trade Center, 30–35, 41
Wright, Frank Lloyd, 42